C. Peterson

MEDITATIONS OF THE MAGI

iUniverse books may be ordered through booksellers or by contacting:

iUniverse
1663 Liberty Drive
Bloomington, IN 47403
www.iuniverse.com
844-349-9409

ISBN: 978-1-6632-4184-9 (sc)
ISBN: 978-1-6632-4183-2 (e)
Library of Congress Control Number: 2022912317

Print information available on the last page.

iUniverse rev. date: 07/19/2022

Exordium

In Him
with Him
through Him
as truth in grace
three unto one Triune
mysterious unity in face
from blessed heart's holy cocoon
too soon beared poor in physical place
of chosen relent unto semitic ascendancy.

Let now thoughts and engaging words flow freely
unmerited sorrowfully so or otherwise written unably
set to play in sooner past events all marked diligently
in events to be told in script yet to be written sacrosantly
written renditions times descriptions some inferentially

Thoughts now of good intent and toward serenity of senses relaxed
finding moments of historic places imagining wrapped by shrouds.
pity not the one to uncover the good made foul by high hopeless fear
efforts reward offers sacrosanct honesty in finding of long sought truth.

We always wary for snares bandits bad persons and bad food
prayers to enlighten hidden dangers always near to bear merit
so to false words and foul intrigues corrupting well ment action
fighting through fired by light of truth ever seeking to belie the lie.

Being well trained and tested for offense and defense
faith esteemed in daily encounters easing efforts to cope
avoiding entanglements of love amiss or love by trick
honesty of heart and mind and kindness wins the way.

Come where good will be welcome
belief in true events unvarnished
following a straight course unique
one aids two so each aids three.

Again and again with wonder
compelling in the telling to writing
then the knowing of truth prophetic
now showing requested participation
ride the path of the singularity writ large
these are parts of love's greatest true story.

Balthazar dealing with transport and timing routes
Gaspar assembling all logistics including papyrus
mine the role of raconteur and correspondence
moments of challenge express different brothers
some reveals are assembled at much later times.

I, being the last foremost acolyte of the Magi Malchiour
named Tangentus the following compulations are mine
based upon documents and adventures after and before
spoken feelings and letters and dispatches all in near time.

The Star

We three
of the East do see
over the Cypress tree
or'e lands of the Semite guest
a sign of prophecy to be revealed
not wavering nor blink and twinkles
a star so steady in the dark blue night
never before seen that close that whole
that near clear and not so high held in mix
others wander dimmer to bright and shimmer
in the night's deep dark wonders all wild aglimmer.

It appeared so clear in comparison near
an oddity within the starry host presenting
a thing unknown yet a thing portentous
a thing mysterious yet a thing offering
of sure location while shedding direction
a star special with its ethereal emanation
aberrant to unnoticed yet its call unabated
clear to we three well traveled and tested.

Devotions ripple round-out-about in crossing demurs
representing the good and the bad in locus high to low
unlike clouds afloat marvelously majestic in its imagery
here to there and everywhere above such a masterly mix
a star falsely hidden beckoned relentlessly a sure direction
unnailed in place shrouded in mystery we proceed faithfully.

Those reading stars unenlightened toward a new light
Mercury to fly fearful news becoming a great moan
recycled gods kings and powers always pretend anew
constructs of belief coming and going here and gone
delivering last news to the ancients' fading abyss.

Stary fates becoming dimmed in the memory of history
mysteries of fate construct and imagined reasons fading
loving a love of ourselves in unstable magical fantasies
seeking to explain impossibilities by hollow falsehoods
fearing the coming and going in carriage of gods' shapes
living a dreaded world of lightening bolts and sea serpents.

We as diplomats need to accommodate many ways
to understand fantastical and fanatical beliefs replete
slow to fast an eye ahead one back wary of false calls.

Three cautious and clever kings of knowledge by faith
evidencing constant learning mistakes of others haste
after usual correspondence in Latin's unyielding twists
to be inexorably drawn from our lush cloistered gardens
eagerly protecting our resolve to learn more from the text
willingly joined in following the mark of the new guiding light.

II

Carrying kingly gifts we left comfort to again outwit treachery
consigned in the traveling coverings of merchant garments
toward a beckoning starlike stare marking beginnings anew.

Navigating degrees of calculations at sea or on worn trails made wide
so thus for us it came to pass those events of fact and faith to place
each gathering at the port well known we often had traveled through
together at the symposiums and seminars Aden Aethiopia offered
the latest in sciences of medicine to mathematics or war tactics.

Melchior from a line of teachers born and raised to rule as Magi of Surat
a bountiful port north of the Ghats overlooking a western setting sun
ruling in service over many years to the Lords of ancient Persis
Gaspar from Abadan at the top of the Sea Persicus
descended from the Magi of Parthian Babylon
Balthasszar Seleucid descendant at Adulus
a man of mental agility in height of Afroism
ruling south of the Kingdom of Axum
at the eastern edge of Africus
each evidencing truthfully
to gain hoary wisdom
to seek knowledge
to council power.

Responsibilities in constancy of royal rule
in service to power through courtly diplomacy
gratefully compensated in the aid of royal works
Roman citizenships by Emperor Caesar Augustus.

Each in wanderings near times of Chu-foo and magic isles
sailed east of Brahma's inside-self ideals by palters and trials
now found following perfectly set light for this purpose to guide by
its radiating fidelity as a precise navigational aid to our new found duty.

III

Friendship reinforced by attending academic seminars and representations
one magi of great east africa cultures and two others of a more eastern mold
brought together over several years of correspondent missions and seminars
knowing the other well specifically by accountable trust gained in difficult trials.

In port to participate in philosophy questing scientific truths of physical functions
earth to air and fire to water of matters visible and invisible in knowledge or faith
prospecting the substance of things hoped for and the evidence of things not seen
reckoning unknowns or following trails well established seeking different possibilities.

This new beginning with two sailing near coastal sands over an oceans course
leaving lush gardens and silent cloisters each renowned as is each respected
each being a patient and devout friend of wisdom with knowledge esteemed
together sapient kings pursuing wonders of nature's natural ever flowing gown
one or other consulted by many for meanings and signs to expose mysteries
all enjoyed investigating portents of fair and foul symmetries for magical effects
doggedly seeking to know the greatest of scrolls and influentially the Hebrew Book.

I

Three days sail along two desert coasts
again traveling to their well attended ports
though Gaspar's stomach mildly complained
traveling winter's cool winds and low warm days.

II

Melchior first among brethren at the symposium to call attention to the aberration
upon appearance of the star we were captured with curiosity as to its presence
no others seemed knowledgeable or caring of its sudden appearance or importance
just another unknown light in a night sky of space previously dark now illuminated
not a matter of astrological significance and not part of any known celestial sign.

Mostly distractions for more earthly matters busily fomenting the sophist's ascendancy
money and lush comforts with foods of distractions in warm snuggery clouded interest
a stretch of imagination to think of it beyond being just another un-notable rogue visage
invested rehashing answers to answers and novel inventions for pleasure and wealth
these times being kind in noting most thinking the immensities of themselves so bright
unable to care for a little bright light uniquely steadfastly alone in some sole confirmation.

Undeterred we three felt something more than illumination by chance circumstance
only we discussed it's amazing presence as a pretext newly reflective of prophecy
to us this new light proceeds a portentous event about to occur deserving attention
knowing comets came and went and stars twinkling held wavering track or phase
nothing new under the sun yet that all things change in never ending eternity of hope
now invested by the necessity to reexamine references in the prescient Book of Isaiah
such a heavenly creation in gift of something thought ever lost to the cruel world of man
a new hope finding placement in the night sky by the form of a star's unwavering presence
announcement by the Ancient One's illuminated prescience which is here to be made whole.

We again continued researching all of The Book seeking words from the Prophets
wonders of contextual truth in poetic commands prophetically made undeniable
cross referencing the words of The Book looking for subtle or suggested definition
some striking out like lightning skidding safely through water onto wading flesh.

We read the illuminations to evidence confirmation without doubt or hesitation
prophecies abundantly clear in The Book to ignite essential truth and signs
becoming witness to the confluence of singularities signifying an original event
blind to the moment we put evidence to the test leading the wise unwilling to deny
being the birth of a child marked by God to be the incarnation of a new king.

Our course to be Aden north by sail then land north to Mare Internum west to Caesarea
as paying merchants in simple garments to Arabian caravel speeds then horse to camel
gaining time we followed worn tracks to Pelusium guided by faith in prophetic direction
moving with calm determination and no hesitation or uncertainty for homage of gifts.

III

Leading it appeared near centered on low horizon
becoming clear evening blushing in the red sunset
to me its draw presenting perfectly projecting lines
expressed linear perfection for us to follow direction
closer it soon bore a well defined radiance in aureole
a cross-like premonstration of a glowing manifestation.

We could almost feel a ethereal emanation manifest
an aspirate resonance intensifying a clarifying purpose
with cooler slow motion desert air above sandy gardens
allowing cold comfort smelling camels growling caravan.

Designed faultless its appearance condensing meditative emotions
a precedent signal announcing change of ways new to the Book
portening events in the converse each to the other of great changes
new meanings exchanged one to the other around campfires.

We agreed from the start that this star burns to incite
to action under that faithfully aged light resplendent above
questions pregnant by enigmatic presence of the guiding star
that hanging cross-fired pendant uniquely calling us three.

The star's surround seemed to be guarded by sentinels of ambient twinkling stars
gaining navigational point traveling by triangulating stars designed to test locations
using geometric calculations by day and exceptional celestial knowledge by night
sailing or riding to walking miles maintaining course toward the star's exact claim.

Added references heralded obliquely to epoch past of Adam and Eve's sin so vast
confidence in The Book assuring us that a confluence of prophecy was at hand
guiding us on the journey being awed by the star's unblinking heavenly quise
knowledge of purpose our oblation would be a pilgrimage to future realization.

The steady unblinking brilliant star holding stable on point quilting we each to gain its mark
aspect of heavenly prism diamond fine being a harbinger of this birth of a new born king
its urge a silent beacon clarion call by the eternal omniscient creator to a band of brothers
messaging from a deep ancient past to portend a new lens for new thoughts and new ways.

It radiates a sublime mystery as aid in lifting the weight of travel from body and mind
selfless curiosity confidently uplifts our hearts for occasional feelings of spirited grace
allusion rent asunder expressing truth by its pure light for assent of new beginnings
something from the light unto each Magi rendering that which will never be the same.

I

Melchiour recalled more of their venture at Aden a dependently joined marked imperative
recollecting sort of like three small streams calmly connecting in the pale moon light
confluences flowing toward a meeting of new coursities questing a fortunate destinity
the timing seemed a planned accident interrupting our uneventful and comfortable luxury
humping by faith hope and charity, rocky sea boat and soft sand to stone hardened pathways
in pursuit of the unknown which of course our talents spoke to but not like this for unpaid fee
there would be and was no hesitation against any deviation forecasting a lost presentation
still there was interruption of usual intemperate events flowing into unsought soft commands
becoming a beguiling quest and by time we gained the offering as being solemn obligation
in a stretch sense becoming an uncle or friend each bearing a gift to births' effusive honey.

Gaspar and I arrived from the east on a double masted high sails thirty cubits ship
two from east of the Syrian Desert and one from the lands east of the Nile River
magi Balthassar traveling from east Africa toward this early winter symposium
no strangers to Aidan's measurably magnificent place harboring many a pirate eye
drawn together in common purpose for knowledge in sciences and philosophy
each seeking the draw of experiment and learning new findings of fact or not
leaving safe harbors of refuge and a world of privilege in satrapy by royal decree
partners unfolding secrets newly veined speaks much of the Ancient One's strength
the evidence was compelling and the facts above heavyweight clinched any doubt.

I

Aiden's strategic port is hustle and frequent disorder due to so many a merchant ship
the selling of slaves and animals and offering astrology to coffins and tricks to trade
its fishing craft, its moving measures, weights, rates, and various slippery coinage
much of sorts and crates with all types of goods and clothing by color and style
things topped, tipped or haved, cut or cured; hustled, carried or abruptly rolled.

By days always learning more for testing in myriad ways few so strange
we had miles to go from Aramaic to cultures Semitic in ways unique
when ensconced we summed up efforts round Adin's strategic port
built of mud and straw huts then to buildings of wood and stone
close in to settled wharfs at-bay with up tight waves of force.

Near the merchants`ships and fishing craft all their moving parts
the ports' measures, weights, rate and sort, delivering goods
tipped or halved seeking almost honest exchange of profits
the smells and banter among the depth of human barters
near about shouts and shoves and fishy hand shakes
the magnificent buildings and palace-like houses
there was much to comment upon these waters
to grouse about and swear fluently of sewers

the port central about for all in's and out's
sharply tipped waves bowing to winds
sea salt in air on any day of delights.

Such action in aid to travelers afar as one from Oiv
seeking spurious ways to cast out demons and oafs
another being a methuselah mountain hermit gone by
in retrospect created as though anew placed in front of you.

A port landing near wild flower, reed, succulent prawn, and piles of fish
maintaining life and limb each arrived seeking how to command privilege
known of foul and deadly deeds we avoided mixing with its hustle and hurry
merchants trading honest effort while others on cunning or theft always by lie
each met the tides and tests of time to gain their place and where to safely rest
we traveled northwest joining privileged comfort at a home of a wealthy merchant
attentively engaging others in welcoming various studies of things worldly or abstract.

II

Balthassar joined by land traveling east to Aden
who sought ways to heft diplomacy and tactics
meridian benighted blessed of vigor and zest
related to Nepenthe of dark and distant fame
known to times of Amenhotep and Nefertiti
those who knew royal life's power to take.

Gaspar joined by seas westerly to Aden
who tuned ways to negotiate healing hate
crested by light brown to amber colored skin
eyes more oval than African deep dark round
leader in structured works and winning tactics
a champion who also dilutes suffering and pains.

III

It was at Aden we first took note of the steady star uniquely rendering its presence
realizing none had any previous knowledge or known mark on its astrological place
others primarily engaged in the prerogatives offered by the privileges of high status
except we three magi others were destined to avoid and dismiss it and unable to see.

The star attracted us of possibilities visible in the accuracy of its stable signature
we searched The Book to find some meaning of a stars referenced new presence
knowing well how to cross-reference we then engaged a cascade of prophecies
words by a grace of getting begged resolution through to its direction not purpose
we became committed to knowing what of its projecting hovering to announce
we became committed to determine by witness to prophecy this star's presence
we believe soon we would know that to follow this pointer leads to a new beginning
our faith in the Ancient One would require oblation greater than that for king David
religious facts prompted by prophecy portended an event by birth now in a new way.

Positions of early morning stars were used to mark pilgrimages course
through the night always the star beckoned and corrected orientation.
faith tempered the pace seeking that which evokes such human relation
this heartfelt journey wrapped in clusters of blind truth must be miracle
mile by mile shuffling to rocking on hard and soft ground cold air around
whether walking or riding the effort was not short on the time appointed
from start toward finish a mark here a way there aided a resettling pace
traveling light on the awkward gentility and beast of burden humped camel
most generous offering wool, meat, milk and a rocking ride in battle or sleep.

IV

Gaining port of entry at grecian Caesarea
each presented royal Magi credential pass
two from the Persian near east to tribal India
one east of the lands Africus near up to the Nile
mentoring the power and golden history of Kush.
Africanic to Aramaic to cultures Semitic among many
powerful worlds mighty and magnificent and dangerous

Now magi travel horizons near shadows of perfidious acts
one who appears in false disguise minions helped below
always friend costumed in truth by pomp and power to hide
hate spread by chimeric contrive with arrogance and pride
under swirls and twirls of cloaked sincerity hiding ugly lies
we know Caesaris history as costumed truth only to pretend
feather crested men seeing beauty's best ignorantly ravaged.

All have been afraid amazed near crazed by doing nothing
we did out play the laughing witch and her assuming way
each knew of ugly deeds and murderous powers' intent
events that which will not relent scheming for greed
of that which is friend and fiend costumed as truth
truth for lie by unholy cabals of no lament or pity.

Next there was that of a malevolent king suspiciously requesting our presence
we had no business or advisement for him so this was a unwelcome diversion
receiving us in accord to status of royal privilege having authorities of interest
welcoming as valued quests who's travel in Judea were of keen interest to him
his wayward world of deviations and excesses evidencing greed wrapped in lies
offering all and any comforts while plying feigned care and concern to advantage
achievements mandating perversions of Hebrew religion promoting its subjugation
a master artisan of hubris, falsehood of face and conscience of rank callousness
his reputation preceded him with it's smell of wine rotting meat flowing from his lips
his is of a dark and fearful mind with wider considerations of a Roman nightmare
overarcing ruthlessness as a fearful dragon hidden under color of purple robes.

Wicked Herod Antipas learned progeny of Herod the Great builder of jewish slavery
constantly requiring words to outwit a fox of considerable size physically and mentally
a fox of a king offers deceitful temptations from a disturbed spirit propositioning advantage

interrupting to assay our last miles to include foiling this unholy King's fraudulent tests
one who exiled the evil one's breath while minions courted discord with death
enhancing cheating or lies and thievery to gain gold and power passing fault elsewhere
paramount obscenities chosen to fill the self-made voids always by violation of power
fearful in a desert of decaying love by jealousies tempering that grant of an Ogre's hate.

Once again we feared his instability and loathed him as he choose not be redeemed
he would not forbear killing innocence to regale in grasp of insatiable greed for power
hate and fear embolden his self interests wasting our time as we could not aid him
a mind to embrace sin for gain of false value or shedding the blood and the life of any
terror of low conscience hiding under smiling pretence of mutual concern and careing
devouring apples to harvest the wood then draining the wells of others to save his own
unholy deeds by place peaceful made terrible by him then to die a foul body and mind.

Knowing well of this king's notorious past acts we deflected our true course
usefully intimating keeping our minds on diplomatic obligations in attendance
cloaking a passing reference to some new born child at a little known place
any further disclosure would merit a threat requiring immediate reprisal
giving little of this and less of that knowing this king destroys any challenge.

We magi held our confidences warey of his well woven snares
professing ignorance in want of knowledge concerning fur trading
after introductions and dinner an area was cleared for entertainment
we disguised our purpose reflecting our attendance as owed courtesy
that we were acting under mercantile license for cross-dealing currency
our destination was Jerusalem after which on to Demascus and southeast.

We spoke generally about machinations of trade in the art of exchange
having dealt with Herod by trade greed and suspicion always preceded
each knowing him by reputation and interaction always wary of his mind
defensive deflection aided by talking around prophesy without any specifics
knowing we couldn't expose our true destination under that light so clearly fine
seeking to mark a place showing ways which can be followed, we demured.

V

Spending little time as possible without disturbing royal animus
we took our leave during the dancing by professing a need for rest
morning light begged securing provisions and resuming our travel
knowing something exalted may render events of greater proportion
our departing trail disappeared into many marks of a camel train
near twenty Bactrian and donkeys loaded with trading goods
goods from Damascus and beyond the Levantine expanse
near cedar wood so required from its place so desired.

More occasioned by cold winds or fire bereft of wood
when nightly wrapped in soft cloth and cowled hood
we each talked of the main goal plans and firm hopes
assurance all's well to then become settled quitely fire out
animals tethered we embrace the coolness of desert nights

having gone southeasterly toward our first nights' encampment
our two poled tent for a welcome sleep closer to our only near goal
next day we turned southerly more acutely aware of marked location
then a day riding on camels to quietly arrive near star's exact sentry
in evening light moving slowly we silently approached Bethlehem village.

I

In the beginning the light ignited from the book
as we began to seek covenant's prophetic hopes
we traveled toward that mark where such could be
relentlessly moving forward morning through late day
magi tasked diplomat can advise a excellent outcome
in this we were driven to see that which others could not
being well aware of soothsayers dark arts and magicians
others who see shrouds alive like mysteries in fog or clouds
by a trance some would speak of many intelligible possibilities
enraptured seeing justice clothed in sheer and slightly torn drapery
capturing solutions engrossed in fa lse science and phantasmagorias
often saying all's the better by some mirage of various deities alighting
refusing to see the safe harbors' satisfactory truths and avoiding shrouds
though inquiring magi in our way have long studied bathed in nearby shadow
of candlelight to aid enlightenment and of sunlight to expose the interminable lie.

We knew astrology and the passion for readings
following prophetic truth was no bar as way thru
we knew of Gilgamesh and other tragic plays
of phantastical ways for false passion anyday
our one recurrent fear of some false move
assuring the unknown is never 1st play
who's future we knew not rise or fall;
will be on those he knows and others by surprise
one who's wisdom and word foretells eternal devise
we traveled unimpaired by that which was unperfected
chasing a nascent future possibility of a hopeful future
to reimagine something of a world missing and lost
one never before seen or known under the sun
it offered heartfelt spontaneous infusions
dreams without false illusions
truth without doubt
a child proclaimed
a star emanations
a hope renewed
it's never before
it's known anew
it's ever to know.

Cross of light
t'was no doubt to mark
our rouse from lands near about
presenting heavenly bright explanations

we three wise men sought to offer confirmation
so others might hear this story then others would know.

Deciding on our own way
we traveled early on cool sands
on paths worn warm in heat of the day
by fox and faith well plied before exact plans
prophetic truth where we hoped it lived and lay
a child so prophysized and professed as now born.

II

Cross of light
it twas no doubt to mark
heavenly visitations shadowed light
we three wise men sought confirmation
by prospect we knew it to be an original truth.

Still the star seemed to appear preface
a fundamental force to mark historic place
to show the dark one wrong and light anew
in the deep dark blue its beams were unmoved
beckoning us join our crossing course face to face.

It's star-like emotive bleeds protective aura
to we who see among all not so sighted
see the birthright of prophecy
it's holy fruition and fusion
truly preternatural
ought to be three
indivisible
as one.

III

To action
now I Melchior
by an overarching
gray wall in valley shadows
again with sunset so to beware
secretly we three of low pretension
dressed in convention of local custom
cut by invention resting near a barreled peak
encamped near their gained goal in months to hours
near the wild seed plants flowering next to a moraine
level ground near potter's all mixed clay cemetery
just before sunset on the first day of the week
three wise travelers attending to our destiny.

Near exact to the place and best eye point
unpacking tent and oil lamp and dry meat to eat
unloaded pack animals soon resting afore safe sleep
I privately quitely communed in prayer near others away
day ride by winter night to arrive under zenith of sentinel star
knowing our early morning intent and direction after encampment
sleeping well before sunlight next morning then to a lingering warning
guide star barely lite becoming a final vanishing pin point then to be gone
a prophecy star pulling forcefully greater then even of wars unkempt strategy
route to Ascalon to Thebes and sea Arabicus and home becoming ambassadorial.

IV

Arriving well after sunset without incident near the village of Bethlehem
traveling the routine distance nearly food abstained by greater anticipation
marking movements without excessive objection from camels or mules
they dismounted securing their five animals by ropes on weighted rocks
well after twilight successfully muscling up our two poled traveling tent
watered and fed as animals needed to bed but not yet we for any rest
then silently walked the southern verge of the little grouping of homes
the low and square to rectangular sparse village homes with lamps alight
a smell of lemon trees then clay shards piled wide behind a potter's house
in anticipation of location they sought direction by approaching a local Inn.

There questioning the only local village inn keeper
feigning we were traveling merchants in need
seeking to find wanderers of new born child
a husband and good wife newly arrived
responding he pointed to a small barn
resident two days recover of birthing.

Only I had spoken to the Inn's owner
pointing to a small barn like structure
confirming therein a boy is newly born
as there is no room at his crowded Inn
he gave a granted accommodation in aid
two in dire need these cool dark blue nights.

We paid cost to quiet our presence
the innkeeper content in receipt
leaving him a forgetful mystery
inattentive to we merchants
abated of anymore interest
he closed the sturdy door
we simply turned away
marked steps to meet
ancient possibilities.

V

We turned away from the Inn keeper's locked door
walking forward only then exposing royal clothing
soon to see a subdued golden hue from a window
a light in a deep dark blue night for each to prepare
confirm a quest as first witness to prophecy exposed.

Prophecy mentions no sword bearer
impoverished at birth enables little power
a scene viewing child not likely to command
weighing inheritance calculated in low exchange
mother and father clothed in rugged cloth uncolored
noting sparse goods and a donkey as collateral promise
all pointing to inevitable probabilities barely above poverty.

Once engaged we learned much more
though first presenting like criminals in flight
anyone who quickly judged became blind to care
their simple happy life here hid more reason to hide
bearing divine obligation the like of which is unknown.

No drop of fear here
that night near the manger
adoring him at a perfect moment
never to see him again so beautiful
prophetic truths made whole in flesh
laying asleep as an all too common babe
a child of low birth now living near poverty
he becomes a powerful new king yet to know.

I

We bearing devine oblation of some useful worth
now cast in a picture with labor as only birth right
our quickly judging interest turns to irreverence
quickly we became engaged as drawn to effects
their simple good spirit showed much character
first proper address simply to ease perceptions.

Humbled by attendance of divine providence
not to involve ourselves much beyond ourselves
ours was not to exaggerate or enjoin in fashion or form
ours is to deliver a message wrapped in notable packages
we kings uniquely the messengers and proudly the message given
under a divined persistent unyielding consistent presence of that star.

We are acknowledged sapient Royals in service to royal power and wealth
'tws fact at Adin we concluded devine prescript not being happenstance
perhaps presence and actions were in fact preordained by the Ancient One

we knew we saw we simply grasped facts being new and not without faith
at Adin we sought facts of divine prescript not those of fools and folly
faith in the Ancient One in ways knowing such works are not negotiated
facts of faith strengthen prophecies' realization being witnessed by others
future acts in ephemeral whispers temporal to soon or too late and then gone
here attestations could not be shaken or discharged from prophecies' realization.

II

On a cold night a new born child lying on straw in a simple crib
safely covered in cloth sleeping quietly in a lowly wooden creche
a protecting warmer air from a small rock surround encircled glow
three attentive shepards shyly standing quietly further from the light
close company by barn animals of lambs and donkey and ox all silent
new child's father near in the eternal starry-eyed cheer for grant all is well
mother well past moments of pain to gain her miracle of life's greatest joy.

They were amazed or befuddled or astonished and troubled
wondering what of we three Magi bearing gifts for presentation
valued gifts brought from storied lands quitely bought unnoticed
intentional gifts of merit for hide-a-way storage foiling plundering;

Nothing preternatural expressed of the child
a babe fully predicted by God's mighty refrain
prophets saw facts in a devine revelatory way
all very natural in a barn of heaven's blessing
not to be different as to any child growing up.

III

Acknowledged as respected Magi in service of kings to influence results
facts gleaned at Adin concluded devine prescript and not happenstance
in retrospect our actions and presence preordained by the Ancient One
grasping faith in prophecy being called and led not by established fact.

At Adin we made what we could of that by presence undoubtedly devine
our faith in the Ancient One in all ways His works being non negotiable
facts strengthened through prophecies' realization as soon witnessed
not of future acts by ephemeral whispers to soon to late and then gone
testament could not be shaken or discharged of prophecies' realization.

We did not travel this distance to speak and run
not to fail by measures of three and insult done
in conversation each of us by age would engage
even short time all was no matter of worrying length
we would end generously on the half moon's passing
leaving we stood together in ending a mystic mission
its residual commands presenting questions yet to be
start to finish a sense of joy in being together near birth.

II

We never forgot that heighted exhilaration the likes of which was never felt again
in the mystery of our summons we thought wrongly in understanding presence
leaving I humbly asked what of his plans he wisely confined to rabbinical sacrifice
not knowing of their Egyption interlude reappearing after the death of King Harod.

Balthassar Adjunct
(written conjunctions to Melchior)

In the going Gasper went to the Innkeeper settling any debt
traveling unknown sureties aided our distance well figured
overall each had traveled long and hard for heed of knowing
bringing something uniquely bestowing ecumenically willing
just right in perfectly woven saccular cloth princely wrought.

Our greatest homage then began toward an out-building barn
we sought him well and true now carrying our gifts of adoration
several steps out we abruptly halted without whisper or comment
reaching near the small barn so as to gain its solid entrance door.

In customary notice for want of entry to alert our present zeal
three times knocking at the steady wooden door holding tight
in the name of revered Melchizedek and by Solomon's seal
humbly we three men of peace seeking entry this cold night
gentiles of note on an urgent course seeking true revelation.

A mild confident voice from within assured a welcome place
once inside none unknowingly were witness to a recent birth
entering we saw little of comfort in aid of such a trying event
there were supplies of simple foods and an amphora of water.

Each astonished to confused to wonderment at our appearance
truly an oddity of impossibilities any one magi let alone three
everything centered toward the child for purpose of oblation
Balthazar spoke of the magnetic draw by prophetic forces
Gaspar of faith in the all mighty Ancient One and always the star
presenting gifts of high order and meaning to a now realized new king
rightful presentations in welcome celebration for husband and mother.

All this in a simple and solidly constructed animal barn of no consequence
the new born child cradled in simple solidly built creche of no exception
held in a apparently quickly constructed cradle for all within a calm aura
staring in attendance a black shadowed bull and a dappled graying goat
three sheep herders one old and two younger most attentive to the babe
a small stone around wood kindling alighting twenty feet into shadows
all chosen to certify by witness to a king of prophecy made newly alive
sleeping in what appeared to be a quickly assembled wooden cradle
exhausted parents looking at a singular greatest miracle interrupted.

All now alert in a cocoon of calm comfort by grace of intimacy
we humbly with royal elegance kneeling to introduce ourselves
culture and learning from Africa to Assyria both high and low
we diplomates and advisors in aid to enlighten kings or queens
magi come from distant lands selflessly following a guiding star.

Initially astounded, astonished and amazed, even befuddled
magi three separately distinct distant lands paying homage
learning each name that of Mary and Joseph looking befuddled
carefully surveying our presence projecting cautious eyes brightly
all resting in a calming surround of security in ethereal campfire glow.

Obviously this was indeed a family of low order and no import
no camel nor horse or mule soon to aid transport of greater load
told their pack is not but a lowly donkey of least expense for travel
no doubt our gifts would be bartered to gain safer use and comfort
oddly no smell of usual rank animal odor in such barns' typical usage.

1

Faith guided fact in bringing this new born king now glorified in a place of poverty
we three by presence of place knew well how to give homage to a new born king
forward three steps then bended knee to the ground setting royal gifts prominently
greeted by surprise and bewilderment of such newly consequent unexpected offerings
humbly presented gifts of esteemed value to a king of type whose value is yet unknown.

Mother, father, shepard's and we three awed so near the exceptional
guided to witness a moment we all celebrate as wondrous and joyful
a singular unifying loving event now animated by fatigue of birthing
a place of grace as an extraordinary expression abiding spirit and faith.

As travelers seeking a new king we scrutinized this lowly place of poverty
no veils of power and no silken rugs or numbered attendants nor food of delights
there was overriding sense of a greater oblique resonance by a heavenly presence
something beyond the well practiced Semitic sensations of a magi's silent meditations
sensations greater than past enthralled enlightenments' feelings in courtly gifts displayed.

Out from trapped tightly wrapped carrying bags
not letting the now freed satchels touch the ground
we each removed our simple woolen cowl and robe
quickly dressed in packed chlamys of arabesque flow,
presenting royal mark in exquisitely purple linen and lines.

High rank dyed cotton and silk with woven strands of silver
court raiment showed clear in truly magnificent investment
only at times most solemn austere or for royal presentation
a flourish in a nondescript manger at most sympathetic place
byzantium and nubian and arabe majestically to pay homage
royal gifts to this new child promised becoming some new king.

Our faces and hands uncovered under the deep dark blue night
each difference in the flickering light round the wooden creche
showing of their ebony and amber and olive sun darkened skin
well blended around a newborn king melding royal introductions
as we each representing gentiles stepping forward in turn by age
each explained travels and intent assuaging doubts of ill purpose
to be present at the revelatory mystery of a new king in the making.

We felt an air of privilege being so near such unique presence
near by animals and beasts of burden and shepard's plight
all surrounded by a comforting oddly extended ethereal light
a glow wondrously greater than a small stone-bound fire
unconstrained by any effects from embers kindling glow
darkness beaten back by some luminous extension.

Among animals and shepherds and a momentary watermaid
time suspended while we relaxed in a haze of growing euphoria
there seemingly emanate a whispering sound of unseen beings
a immaterial presence accompanied by waves of muted vibrations
unseen wonder and joy in a swirling warmth of perfumed breath
the greater moment projecting in each a renewing sense of joy
a overarching vail of security offering some kind of ethereal privacy
enveloped periphery in exhilaration of place in comfort of serenity
an intimate cuddle of esteem sincerely enveloped by joy of no rein.

II

That is as each felt it and saw it in its mystery and calm simplicity
later speaking about a background of constant mingling euphony
though diplomats all the while we were near weakness in reverence
aided by the innocence of this new born child lying sinless in a creche
what portends the future of this child in grace by good spirit's intentions.

Having knocked asking entry demonstrating our good and honorable intent
allowing we Magi welcome then honored by our surprise salutary presence
staring in near disbelief asking what guide brought us to this outside place
Joseph, husband of Mary, first softly spoke to us in a rustic Aramaic dialect
prominently bringing close attention and concern to our purpose of presence.

Mary poised calm and considerate and acutely wary
such evident poverty resting aside a new born king
having risen from bended knee I spoke first and for each
blessed husband orthodoxy by prophecy we seek to testify as true
our following of a star singularly expressing an event of importance
the inn owner directed us to you and blessed wife's shelter for birthing.

We being inexorably drawn by forces greater than ourselves to be witness
king's being gentiles for witness to prophesies' promises now made whole
warranted to carry out without hesitation or explanation that which is deemed
royal gift's to a carpenter and a blessed mother for a poor family's comfort.

Standing comfortably back after offering our gifts properly to the father
graciously welcoming acceptance of gifts of oblation were well taken
being somewhat oblique speaking of reasons concerning the gift's,
prophecies definitions are usually not inherently well defined.

Time by more than minutes extended genial conversation
for all it was not a few minutes of a short moment in time
upon leaving we noted the passing time by moonlight
unpressed time gratefully caught our hour taken.

We understood little then knew more
they though burdened but not bent
both evident strength of character
that class of constant struggle
works catch as catch can
selfless love emanates
portent by prophecy
child of promise
realized anew
questions all
gratitudes.

III

Ours was not an aside safely posed as a delegation of passing transit
premonitions of intrigue could not be dismissed lest we be taken as remiss
measured by probabilities some evils of hell being loosed without hesitation
knowing of many a kings' fears of losing power for naught of drastic action
fearing of a corrupt king well familiar with the lures of evil's hideous dance.

After oblations to this perfect creation of future unknowns accepting this prophetic beginning
perhaps a light in the darkness of myriad wrongs to render equity unto the tempest and fray
all here near a new hope of peace prevailing in a dangerous world of war and misery so diverse
creation of something holy now surrounded by feelings of ethereally glowing motions flowing.

Undue excess excluded by the calmness of place
effusive joy of family huddled in births' veneration
all bearing witness to the miracle of new born life
birth's release and mark of truth to probabilities
prophets of The Ancient One carry high weight.

I

There were those doubts
Balthassar's recurrent why
this age to bring such truth alive
net of circumstances cast so wide
unleashing science and philosophizes
thinking we could retract course to hide
to turn away from such an outright oddity.

What of the star and why we three chosen to proceed
having not shied from involving ourselves in local histories
never hubris could we imagine such strength of prophets call
no entertaining doubts thinking we might be lost over our heads
confusion or fear could not assemble themselves to thwart travel
to we three the die was cast by faith in the Ancient One's tall truth.

Closing the distance looking upward to claim positioning
then upon the exact location for chosen privilege face to face
our interest ending at a near outpost of a lightly referenced village
faith strengthened continuous attraction ending on no fools errand
inside of such epiphany any doubt evaporated in form and manner.

As we left I turned to lastly view each of those three ever locked together
turning my gaze toward the babe's mother's hand rocking the cradle,
marveling on her serene countenance during this abrupt entry
asking for the child's name she replied he is named Jesus
in response speaking that name we now shall not forget
saying we will not forget his name for ever watching.

Rearranged in simpler dress on leaving the area
that place of mystery and stories yet to unfold
leaving something of being the first to know
wooden manger carved into our memory
miracle of birth of a wonder on earth
a magnificent expression of love
burdens of poverty made quiet
truth of prophecy possible
time and place maligned
challenges are replete
lost to any exception
weights unknown
faith will be act
here and now
today he is
future est
to follow.

We three went directly back to our tented area
under a deep dark blue sky heaven rent clear
walking past potter's field of hopes dashed
plans to establish resetting our next path
adeptly disguised to outwit wicked wiles
efforts designed to conceal our return.

Melchiour brought forth a set timed route
Gaspar calculating a cunning retreat
each mapping our course southerly
the black knight designing new fight
keeping our confidences assured
strength in strategies now to act

excellent tactics to bring the win
always first steward to follow
much enriched by practices
backed in many a victory
now a precise way to go.

II

Prepared to leave at first morning light
quietly away from our inclusive interlude
seeing that of which being first written
humbly reverent assembly bitten by fact
leaving unleavened possibilities to follow
also noting that sense of euphoria we felt.

Later meditations aided collected recollections rewritten
remembering expectations seeing that part of prophecy
emotions running the course dismissing failures reach
start to finish our participation was wholly unexpected.

Always after would be moments of joy in the reliving
a singular event becoming incomprehensible possibilities
quietly present a powerful bull is as calm as baby sleeping
another beast unburdened and then alert was a dutiful donkey.

As our invitation so to shepherds quietly speaking near hearing
repeatedly whispering of a heavenly presence showing the way
something of the Ancient One appeared showing them the way
all watching over a flock as we rode to walk towards the light.

Intently excited by a compelling force speaking drawing each near
an elder holding close a young lamb standing near a tethered goat
aside two more young shepards standing back from birth and baby
a recused handmaiden carrying a water jug out the near side door
each to aid the miracle of birth unfolding slipping unto a new world
now made whole by the mystery of the prophecies partly unlocked.

I

Travelers attending duties on first light we closed the small encampment
we took our leave on our camels guiding donkey's carrying fewer stores
following a well planned return for a jog northwest then a turn west to south
soon sailing back to port in a westerly way out from the Province of Judea
hence down to Aden's markets with its far-flung and myriads of merchants
a spirited eminently dangerous port offering sublimely gifted profitable ways.

Always of trade and the bargain for access or denial even for inhuman acts
unguarded grasp of human or not as all things bought or sold secret or not
presenting exquisite colors and languages ranging from complex to pointing

old ideas newly packaged by the smoke of prejudices awaking false beliefs
scientifically firm to exuberantly fantastic guaranteeing a flat or rounded world
dabiler's dangerous use of sophistic ways ending badly one way or another.

Dealers for gain in a place of mercantile entrapments requiring unmoderated doubt
entertaining reason and logic and mathematics of various new inventions are welcomed
conjectures and prognostications and critiques without inherent value quickly dismissed
leary of guarantees wrapped in made-up stories of exploits and adventures requiring cash
a rogue port deserves and serves its questionable reputation without unjust inferences
carpe diem cut the fat and grab the highest return with honest care running speedy away.

Knowing of spies and unsavory minions seeking to strike as vipers
west toward statutes requiring worship in constructs and contradictions
the lingering pull and push of Pharaohs power or the heavy boot of Persia
hope or loss built on shifting sands and hard power dicing actions sways
each delt practiced tricks of trade by advantage of privileged accesses.

Always in a bowing way to many numbered breasts, eye or limb
all the wiles of gods mirrored as drenched in excessives of self
by the four winds each in some way locked in tribal gain or forfeit
Balthassar trained in ancient belief leads two of Zoroastrian lineage
all practiced sages and diviners knowing much of an Ancient One
taking percentages of diplomatic and material profit in kings service.

II

In the port from whence we came soon on Balthassar going East of Eden's lush gardens
Aethiopian interests of a black man physically powerful of mental match to any challenge
indulging Ethoi-nubian's gold and the gardens of east Africa south of the Elephantine Philae
Melchior eastward with Gaspar in company back to Assyrian and Mesopotamia comforts.

Gaspar by sea sailing leagues and his caravan north returning to Seleucia's entrenchments
over years we three with or without diplomatic privilege maintained interest in the child king
in aid of spy scribes we pledged continuing discourses thru usual scrolls correspondence
each having numerous well placed informants aiding in diplomatic and mercantile concerns
receiving usual reports sent along the epic and dangerous Arabia and Persian coastal seas
stringent seas guided by wisdom's forecast of night winds clear and red mornings warning.

GASPER'S ADJUNCTION
(reminiscences to Melchior)

I

Older by prospective meditations and reflections concerning events and travels
the next thirteen years Melchior purposely met some few trusted Hebrew agents
agents familiar to persons with hairs curved round or straight or eastern black oval
enduring many burdens heaving hardships weight and too many a day of lean plate
to abate and scare away false dealings often bungled against truth's hefty strength
being enjoined by the humble or to endure the assuredly proud one helping one not

each plenipotentiary gaining good to exemplary results through tempered experience
informing on the extrapolations and interpretations of religions confrontations to cover.

Trade being central to purpose and talents and wisdom royally compensated
asked to explain for others that which others could not explain for themselves
few stood even and upright in temperment others knew plenty about nothing
assignments included royal harems to fleeing fierce events of warfare's trials
smelling strange people in palaces to caves to pens or arena for bloody offerings
all in a world populated by hellish things of seamen's serpents and furious Gods
this one worse than that one and some other worse than those over there or them
always fingers pointing at this or that or these and those as best against the rest.

Together sooner or later recalling the events drawing us forward to be under it
unlike a moth or cupid's arrow hitting a random mark we by purest light beckoned
drawn by a force of nature directing and inescapably demanding attention to a star
a very important event foretold of in the Book hoped for in singularity of Judaic faith
forces not unknown that could fracture time to remake that which was our lost grant.

Always back to inebriation of heightened agreeable conversation
and more tales of the trip's mystery and it's reflecting affirmations
perchance to esteem our services helping and not causing harms
intermitable convolutions of transgressions and retailed temptations
confirming affirmations by not mismarking love and avoiding the logic
checking ourselves what and why of the guiding eastward bearing star
to be understood seeking truth by belief and faith in that which is unseen
that star that aberration that perfect creation beckoning resolution so near
communing with philologia grappling that truth to gain reference in The Book
the type of the star and by its draw signaling part of something greater is to be
reflecting on One of long ago once again working His way in time leading we three
the 'Ancient One' who walked this earth in ways known to gain stopping the one below.

As a point of interest there was a solitude which he referenced himself
it was always truly nem dissentient as to any need for quiescent recall
delicate definitions of why it was reflected in that special time to place
projecting that which was already claimed this time he again appears
not one over-spoke any other all speech being exactly point of extant
be or not our feelings corralled by faith all shows the presence of Him.

The perfume of newborn life lingered in the air on this being the day after birth
again to emphasize effect of a surround excluding all other smells possibly near
to that exception and its discomfort was added some contemporaneous mirth
soon to become settled and in trust of each so to our words were easy to hear
Gaspar a master of Indian spices and Orient tea was pleasantly overwhelmed
each to feel the unique engrossing effect of the manger area so perfumed.

Gasper wrote how it was in that time at that place of its confident revelations
Mary and Joseph amazed looked dazed and astonished as to our royal presence
we revealing garments of magnificent and royal presentation kneeling then in sitting
to bow to each presenting our royal gift's calmly speaking quietly of prophecies' truth
asking by what name the new born child shall be known so engraved in memory Jesus

in going speaking directly it will not be forgotten by name he shall be remembered by us
stepping out on turning back again relaying Herod lerks may prudence lead you safely away.

II

Intrusive we lingered awhile in talking
resting presenting valued aeromatic gift's
high content stamped small gold coins
all valued for enabling them alternatives;
easily hidden and leniently exchanged.

Properly kneeling in requisite benefaction;
genuflected to present gifts in homage
hope being so near to many dangers
a new king shall render new ways.

A new king gripped by challenges
old fears seek to quickly extinguish
entrenched power will not so hesitate
first to eliminate any such challenge.

III

So as arrived we quietly left that simple village
our disguised purpose was a peaceful exchange
no reason for our place or our notice made in going;
little Bethlehem's appended mark on history showing.

Footing caution we went quietly
into the deep dark blue night
silently going back to our tent
a safe solidly poled necessity
unheard and unseen to others
excepting by the uninterested
rough Inn keeper's bare notice.

All under that star of royal calling
truth to manifest itself from revelation
being there with a special future so new
precipitating a coming of greater inspiration
knowing misadventures are always at the ready.

I

Written anew recalling more not always in customary order
soon after we arrived Joseph magnanimously provided a bench
judging height in equivalence to ourselves to be just about six feet
strength obvious in his wrestling effort while adjusting its placement
his wool overcoat untied showing the covered body of a lean stature.

Otherwise noted we moved into the deep dark blue night silently
pack animals held in place tethered at the ready for morning travel
our normatic tent of comforts and a short night of worries forgotten
Gaspar last to speak before Morpheus' cloak settled the day's deeds
first if no holy fear in life then what of mortals' battle in unholy life of fear
only selfish gain and selfish loss and therein nothing everlasting ever after
so our beneficial gifts to wandering jews' precipitant to concerns of calamity
great dangers now and great dangers after seems the lot of this appointment
later recompositions required additional calibrations for misplaced communications

Gaspar was first to see the light of the guiding star waning in the night sky
a light that infused a magnetic internal grasp leading their itinerant voyage
even now its dimming curiously warming us against a coming cold wind
Gaspar mused perhaps in him is king David's true cost stumbling self to tears
perhaps larger still to rectify some greater transgressions in a fight for limits in life.

II

Continuing compliations written and presented as to all things and ways lettered
Gaspar writes spontaneous refrains this must be some part of the Ancient One
nothing other moves the heavens or animates the certainty of Torah prophecy
this child destined to be a new king of kings is now truth in prophecy dirt poor
a prophecy perhaps of great glory greater than that whichever came before
we magi quietly speaking freely agreeing the sanctity of that simple manger
it is in belief that we three may find truth paying homage to a stronger faith.

Pursued by protocol as constructed we tendered our gifts then conversation
each speaking in order of age and all condensed in the Aramaic language
those ways preceded identifying credentials as presented to the parents
two of Siddhartha's east of the sands One east of a continental divide
vigilant against wayward infraction honoring magi priorities to aid
here encamped near a tent post marking being guided by a star.

Something very unique occurred that deep dark blue night for our instruction,
gifts of honor given as we were enraptured by the exhilaration of mystery
fully feeling extrasensory forces animating light in wisps of substance
a force greater than low fire light effortlessly keeping the dark at bay
a spiritual effect of the event captured by motions stirring unseen,
though worries abound those now disappear assuring all's well
it was something he would never forget of those veiled murmurs.

Gaspars writings recalled comforting warmth at the manger
he professed it was a moment of serene calmness and security
a place of serenity protected by some gift of grace assured in faith
a comforting aura of a presence unrestricted by confines of mortal life
unbundled surreal spontaneous airy flirtations by entities exalting joyfully
joined under some translucent covering cocoon unburdening any selfishness
all in a normal pleasant conversation and by sight well aware of all physicalities
being their forth day past before coming morning to then leave that very next day.

I

Their going will help scramble any of Harod's exposed interests
we chose not to make any reference of our encounter with Herod
during time spent with Herod it is now a game of dog and clever cats
our familiarity with courtly intrigues were not less than as practiced there
we three differentially spoke inferentially about nascent prophesy to Herod
bewildered Herod called counsel priests and scribes to uncover these claims
the Prophets of the Book pointed to Belthleham as again Herod sought our help
by our giving notice he requested our confirmation returning notice of our findings
we assented then ignored it outright acutely knowing the way in and a quiet way out.

Later we learned soothsayers whispered into eager ears warmed by fear
not to worry great king kill them kill them all innocence shall not escape
it has been done many times many ways many places all more like you
not first nor last to take command to demand and harken to a devil's face
none shall remember all soon forgotten disappearing like dust in a whirlwind
prophesy be damned fate riddled by lies to crush threats to take command.

MELCHIOR'S ADJUNCTION

I

Mary and Joseph were astonished by our presence our words and our gifts
our royal presentments royal homage royal acts royal origins unknown to them
our world's were never so close we three blessed to be near those blessed three
twelve years later I by cover of being a merchant pilgrim of normal understated rank
leaving Ostia to the port at Caesarea on a fast single-banked merchant owned cruiser
Harod's master port in glory of Caesar Augustus with its Greco-Roman invasion of Judea
after closing diplomatic works my attention shifted to the Markets and the Temple collegium.

II

To find out about the current status and circumstances of the boy Jesus
now in the thirteenth year past his announced arrival by prophecies incarnate
in meeting secretly arranged by my foremost Judean scribe and principal agent
timing coinciding with the child's development now by obligation year at Nazareth.

III

We sagacious eminent kings from the east traveled kingdoms all around
moving among chief priests or royalty or city kings or dominions unbound
aiding our devotions in seeking truths and assaying mysteries of science
open minded complex investigations or often by simple chance discoveries
learning the mistakes of self always wanting to note missteps of others.

Later after their Judaic obligations I learned of their move to relatives in Egypt
soon after the death of Herod the Great and of their safe return to Nazareth
living in Nazareth the boy would occasionally travel to Esdraela or Tiberias.

I

Now meeting a most trusted scribe soon after the boys thirteenth year
to my correspondent scribe I never need complain of value for effort
always not sharing with him or others events concerning Bethlehem
never verbally or in any writing revealing presence at the manger
also never informing my scribes of purpose or intent for reports
theirs is simply a matter of sending regular informal accounts
my controls avoid missteps involving the boys future events
so any lie is avoided by the greater fear of exposing truth
otherwise its tell me no secrets and i'll tell you no lies.

Reports indicated no hint of transcendent prophecy
nothing to yet inform any further unmasking of itself
encouraging the importance of his familiar reports
in Rome he received a report of riveting interest.

That time while being in Rome he received notice inserted in a diplomatic cylinder
it disclosed an event of interest that had transpired at a Temple collegium discourse
shortly thereafter Melchior left Rome from Ostia to Ceseara on a diplomatic recourse
in Ceseara with business complete he arranged a closer account with his chief scribe
traveling to Jerusalem under guise of a merchant perchance aiding incomplete interests
a fuller account of those meetings follows by senior scribe and he near the Temple cohort
the teachers expressed no doubt in the piety of the boy/man by his knowledge of The Book
asking and knowing showed a devout piousness for interpretations from the master teachers.

II

Moving forward
this light of curiosity
abet learning to beware
after four years living in Egypt
then passing ten years in Nazareth
to be mildly knowing and fiercely loving
there was that time of noticeable transition
that change by presentment hereafter recorded
Melchiour took notice of the boys exceptional day

The Finding

It was related to me that learned men did not ignore him
some engaged him knowing him first as a simple curiosity
he ably related details of scripture and events all by The Book
in ways intimate a marvel to hear no errant sophistic convolutions
no intended diversions or truths twisted aiding prideful presentations
no misguiding of places or times and events all for the truth of The Book.

He was relaxed in an sparsely shaded bisected demilit portico within an outer court
outermost of theTemple surrounded by fortified Roman walls increasingly reinforced
on cusp of manhood the child heard Talmudic interpretations of laws and Scripture
these were serious men doing and discussing serious works seeking God's markers.

He was well versed showing an exceptional knowledge of the Book
there to receive subtle interpretations and inferences for understanding
at one point querying him as to who sent him and simply stating his father
the best teaching locus fathers advocate sending their sons' to engage.

II

As it happened that day his visit was unpretentious and extemporaneous
not contemplated or arranged before or during or after the usual trek south
a brilliant sun moved dim shade over several older men seated or standing
causing the boy often to be cross shadowed under cedar beams of weight
carriage of pillar and post nailed with awning under yawning midday heat.

All enjoying references clear to imprecise and cited for interpretations
he interacted by knowing events or facts and listening to explanations
honoring examples of the Ancient One informing on his children's actions
he knew well the history of Jewish ascendancy chronicled in The Book
wanting explanations to highlight the numerous applications of Judaic laws
responding only when asked giving answers accurately reciting facts.

Listening to their filtered simple to monumental meanings
with Rabbi's among those gathered near the Temple Salem
wherein presenting the comforting majesty of One True God
energized in the certainty of oneness inspiring their singularity
no indifference, no illusionism, no renderings of false deities.

He listened intently to the others most invested the elders and teachers
other small groups sitting on stone or wooden benches or standing about
he brought no particular or noticeable concerns into the fluid attendance
all seeking insights to exact little known facts to anoint themselves in truth
calling forth a union of Biblical history never to be lost in past or near dispairs
ignited by the love of truth full force in seeking their studies of the Ancient One.

No Sanhedrin and no Pharisees in their midst or chose to come near that day
calm discourse brought out equities and logic in interpretations of Biblical truth
all hungry to reflect to meditate to debate to know Enoch's to Abraham's ways
when asked this young student returned answers correct making each word erect
many admitted exceptional knowledge by this new young man not so verbally fair
subjects for attentions to identifications and joy of renderings were well received
under the shadow of the crossed beams present under humility's challenging care.

He bespoke his preface to participate sincerely as I am here to learn of you
more so discourse what of these things of shepherds and kings in The Book.

During his time discussions were spontaneously lively and evenly modulated
any expressions of rivalry dissipated like a high noon hot day run of clouds
vigor excited by the dance of intelligence infused each on turn of subject
historic events ignited interests in stories of pride in its challenges to humility
words and meanings devoid of jealoulsies's exceptual scowls and argument
speakers' enmity by competition's prideful ways were put aside to throw away.

When included the Nasarine was not figgity obtuse or hesitant
thoughtful never losing hold of where he was or to whom he spoke
their laws and of past events beautiful dangerous or well fought
bereft of things known for lifting lies on high to tarnish the covenant
of Hebrew pains and pleasures about where love is never fully fanciful
smiling how Temple butterflies flew by aires of wonder freedoms aside
speaking always about never unknown and ways together ever near Him.

He a youth of promise holding his tack with his own and perhaps some even more
while celebrating those hours at the Temple not realizing his parents frantic search
desperately seeking to see to almost schold to hold to be with him not where they were
fearful of where he might be so young not knowing all the wiles or tests of devil's perr.

I

So
said he,
to each alcolite
as we yearned to learn
of years of historic glories
born studied of Fabula to Ceaser
when richness of agricultura conquered,
and markets from Pythians to Gauls comforted
during transition for chance of idols on to their dying.

So said mentor master teacher Melchiour
in domi' reign of Octavious Ceaser Augustus
from rule of dux Malodorous Perfidious Tiberius
all squalor and wondiferous splendor of Roman realms
and world's curved inference swooned under wandering helmes
little noticed admixed wayward ways of man's incalculable space given

not a sure world nor the best way gaining truth by lies and sophisms of typology
wanderers reigning committed to days of hot toil on footfalls unriven seeking doxology.

.

They began that solemn trek excited on a trail known well to others having the way
each toward some holy presentation of purpose and hope leading to moments of elation
joining thanksgivings and reverences at the epitome of a city ordained and not a circus show
to know this way is not as others have gone along a dangerous rocky dry and dusty road.

Melchior continued to unfold the story of events occurring during his forty sixth year
he spoke more of this poor middling child who would somehow become a king of kings
this child is unique and all so alike in childish things and childish ways similarly refrained
he spoke of a youth moving freely learning the ways of his woodwright carpenter father
as how the boy matured happily doing the good deeds of an obedient son of good intent.
aiding his father at some carpenter's mill obtaining correct types and sizes of woods
by requests of his father he began learning the trade of both rough or finished works
lessons in strength of body and patience of mind for making fine and sturdy constructs
it was a fee for service 'lest charitable necessities or Rabbi's requests dictated otherwise
Joseph's works never evidenced grande or ostentatious effort though such could be done.

This assuredly is hard work and menial reward with greatest joy a simple childhood life.
still at a young age his father knew the boy enjoyed the company of his local brothers
finding ways to test themselves to be best at children's games still loving to be at play
a time and place in manner of things physical not rendered to ubiquitous god's esteem.

It was related as to how his friends and he nonchalantly tricked each other in games
expressions of youth still clothed in innocence with small attention to future endeavors
nothing cast in stone except religion and family and friends on usual visions of greatness
ever mid-morning light of heat or cold these friends of accord tended to many chores.
once in a while just him and his friends playing in open air in fray of common kids' day.

II

Annual unity for three days travel aiding each other along the dusty rocky road
this special journey held them tightly together in a group onward to the Temple
the scribe related more of what of his usual report containing these local matters
saying as was related they moved in a group thick and thin forty three in number
some in slow bunches causing bulges at the front others with dusty ragged ends
all accompanied by the shuffle's of movement and cacophonous clatters and din
there were affable talks amid the children's sporadic excited words and shouts
mixed unmatched hoofed animals' grunt's stirring fies for carrying the goods
mounted with stocks and stores to sell or barter and few things to be gifted.

Still there was time for playing games and tending to traveler's chores
his close friend somewhat unkempt aiding and abetting Jesus' efforts
a dearest helpful friend caught by stumbles and having smiles for truth
speech somewhat slurred by agitation and lungs unrestful as not clear.

Passing three days of camping in sites rugged under the sun's discomforts
wary always of fouled food or faintness and cramp by water made worthless

all pre arranged for three serial camps set under high clear bright moon light
completing close-in camping just outside the City's magnificent wooden gate
nightly wandering invites missteps of concern for closed doors just camels' eye.

Daily admitting staples of beans to dates and flour to wine sacs and few jars of honey
overseers noted entry of all goods mauled by all manner of entrants some turned away
especially sought fruits and vegetables brought to market eatable near blemish free
crossing an entry line of extended pack animals were for safety concerns checked
except for count or type of ownership and health most animals were left untouched
especially sought out were any possible weapons excepting tools of trade or gift.

III

Melchior began to dispose the import of this great city's history and consequence
a history of socially and emotionally excitefully and delightfully ascending conglutination
one of significance for its highs and lows of influential religious impressions and expressions
a place of singularity of the Ancient One glorified by its Hebraic oneness defined in Tora.

A city's central part and place of pilgrimage now marking past wanderings from abyss
aoristic rituals in dispositions and offerings replete with animated enthusiasm at its center
roiled verbal encounters and physical presentments as inviting invocations as burned
crowded squares and streets for passages of diverse commerce or residence and residue
no priestly actions requisite not presenting Torah's written tests of true faith for action.

He related more of that meeting between he and the scribe
hearing and wanting to know more of that humble family band
in caravan traveling miles over scraggy ground and soft sands
wanting to know how prophecy faithfully grows in this man/ child.

I

His age almost set near about thirteen
the boy was graced by a calm even gage
past being a child now a green youth unknown
presenting a lean muscular physique with speed afoot
nascent carpenter's strength gained by his father teaching.

Soon a man by Hebrew command he was sure in stature
innate confident presenting by nature a gentle and kind will
no airs of convoluted pride or false ways spuriously invented
in body and gait unlike his near friend dear friend and best friend
a boy next to the baker who inherited a challenge upon a birth's mix
an uncomplicated soul not much down yet high in trust through smiles.

This friend a younger brother of another's in their tightly knit group
ipsissima verba always truthful soberdown a pleasant disposition
each for each never playing loose making the other for dupe
nor by advantage seeking one for other in selfish divisions

each having that self same ability of constant humility
displayed in all efforts general and genial in affability.

Eschewing any sense of vanity enlightened by compliment
a near expectant shy continence remarkably subtle and gentle
in action or prayer he is covered quiescent in deference to the task
hands and shoulders and arms beginning to show steadfast work ability
fashioned by nascent strengths gained by being a woodwork's apprentice.

In a pilgrimage all efforts come together by the processional journey
there were many to more complaints brought and made mostly settled
for three consecutive days in travel blessed by summer's mild beginnings
the focused purpose and effort is communal yet unusual challenges do occur
worn weary ways tested by errors of chance lead some few uncaged demands
goans or gripes expected some smiles of laughter survived in pliant selfless ways.

Encamped freed by toil done he with others enjoyed communal sport
amiable tests of youthful skill in rompish dance around a lambskin ball
none bested the cavort of friendship strengthened by amiable attitudes
testing good humor on a bad call by resolve not to end in any divisions.
his gradual changes casting good-bye to more childish games and ways.

II

When in company of Joseph and Mary all honesty was unshaven
there fidelity of promise is shared by interdependent inner authority
nothing amis by motions and manners and discourse spoken or not
tangible trust betokens no sense of royal superiority or tricks to trip
complimenting beneficence holding in consideration of no station.

Speech colored his voice a level baritone
a controlled slightly higher pitch for warning
most words undulated in temperate level low tone
emphasis' lowered speech tending to a moderate bass
all pleasant sounds even in its chromatic manifestations.

He exhibited patience and inquisitive deference to others
showing exceptional qualities of good intent and nature
likely uncanny sense led to unwaxing the liar and cheat
by inclination of obvious and overriding pentralia mentis
speaking of conflicts he always gravitated toward equities
avoiding invective expressions as one would avoid plague.

I

Any and all passing cross
ever slowly thru massive Gate
under pediment of carved stone

a city of close smell and rebellious nature
civilized shame tamed man out from the wilderness.

Merchant to celebrant pilgrims with residents numbering in tens of thousands
all could gaze at the wonders of greatness and the long ago remnants of ruin
a city's newly extracted pressured rock erected in sharp smooth constructs
cut stone procured towed floated and pushed over sand and mud and sea
pulled dragged muled and placed in constructs by muscles always aching
rolled slid and hoisted by pulley rope and leverage in magnificent proportion.

A city embellished by mosaics and bright red to brown interlaced roofs of clay and wood
iron made points of filigree on windows and doors posing safety as fortress against night
some few occupants adorned with fine cloth and colored bracelets and hidden weapons
others emanating spectrums of perfumes combed all about each curl and strand of hair.

Markets offering epicurean delights sold or traded by foriegn and local shops or kiosks
obscured fast and loose occupations dealing in all types of activities and merchandise
lodgings to accommodate all complexions allowing for comfort of toilets and bathing
sewered streets and ways for wells and flowing water in an oasis of jumbled humanity.

Always temptations in service to the imagined warmth of cold greed or avarice
panoplies of citizens to serve and salve seeking better prospects and comforts
each their own unique guide wanting though not wholly given to continence
constant undercurrents of resistance to assaults and insults by heretic imports.

Rooftop to sewer rail multifarious manifestations of statutes and rules of governance
contractual centuries as vinculum to the One just beyond the pale of time or place
in body and mind a city of affirmations resident in it's Temple of holy glorification
a people forged and measured by intense strife and their magnificent creation.

A land no more void of histories honest values and highest of fidelities extant
it's rains fall on the good the bad the just and unjust the rugged and the weak
a home to times of histories fearsome marvels and fearsome times yet to be
this place expressing the enmity of man holding its own against a sea of troubles
ports and ways melding challenges of Latinus sea and Graeca's plagiarized past.

Jerusalem centered belief to temperament and practice of their most singular faith
whether safe at home or moving in close presence through city alleys and streets
getting from place to place often appeared like wandering confusion in nearness
the central Temple for prayer and sacrifice ever together hoping God's pleasure
their faith held free securely behind a near impenetrable cohort Roman defense
rough to smooth cut stone protecting outer quadrangalary set walled periphery
designed simplicity of perimeter strengths spectacularly made to win challenges.

II

At the Tabernacle Tent outside the city gates needle closed
each evening Mary and others set the table with Jewish care
he among the more than few all together they ate best of stew

each day they went to market and then to be near Great Temple
on the second day Joseph presented for sacrifice the ritual offering
accordingly a custom of the celebrations all precise and body washed
by the Book and Law and Statues he sealed that enduring Jewish faith
Roman soldiers kept guard and watch on walls and walkways to barracks.

Upon completion of custom celebrations and obligations at tent and Temple
the Nazarene troup assembled all but one for their journey back homeward
brothers and sisters all among the group except the most unawares one boy
going out from the Tabernacle tent area straight back to the Temple gathering.

After preparations the afternoon sun began the four day trek to their Nazarene home
guarded watered and well fed secured animals grunted rolling several wooden carts
pilgrims milling emotions in caravan retracing home their stay of five days ending well
packed and secured preparations for three nights encampments and water and wine
morning of mid-week departing in murmuring roil with some glancing looks backward.

I

Melchior noted to the acolytes how his scribe and paid spies well adhered to facts
doing works knowing that which is found is refined and reported as not embellished
seeking truth needs stay close-onto fact or suffer embrace of poorer probabilities
presentations of fabrications to truth only tighten a woven cloth of speculating facts.

II

After several hours Mary and Joseph secured place in the bulge of convoy
yet their dear only son Jesus was not in or near about that section of line
Mary seeking to find him questioned and searched all those fore and aft
she concerned and Joseph perplexed as they each amplified their worry
friends last saw him in the early morning past he cast a toy to a near child
not informing his intent he turned to round a corner vanishing in the milieu
by accord the caravan continued its slow pace toward the first encampment.

Avoiding paths of innumerable diversions they hastened in gaining reentry
in short order revisiting relatives and friends and places of familiar interest
areas of common shops and muddled markets always seeking known faces
worries magnified by the confusion of possibilities and any untoward dangers
time remaining in light of the first day seeking him was limited to a few hours.

In places unpleasantly dangerous they intently relentlessly had sought him
close after about eight hour's past sunrise on the second day of their search
not finding him after all the anxious time from departing the rambling caravan
now caught in the chaos of multitudes and its manifestly organized confusion
still more worried of far worse uncontrolled darker places hiding malevolent intent
perhaps injured cast aside uncared for by the many hurriedly walking blindly by
after second night and on third day measuring long their parental fears highest

They neared the public entries of the magnificent Herodian rebuilt Holy Temple
frustration amplifying worry inciting more fearful imaginations of him not there.
in their roundabout ways they gavitated inward toward the grandeur of the Temple
together in the heavy air of wet heat passing through the outer pergolas and stalls
edging near the intimate sectional places for seminars or symposiums of debate
at that Most Holy place they captured the joy and relief of finding him unharmed.

A great weight of fear and jerking tensions dissipated when they saw him
they were as happy to find him as he was at a loss of the caravan's leaving
interests of the minds and hearts of the learned teachers overwhelmed many
discerning Biblical history for applications to guide and strengthen its teaching
testing his knowledge of persons to places and times was adjudged exceptional
answers to challenges of fact were well received charging the discourse of debate
glory of place held him in site and inattentive ignorance to caravan's homeward trek.

Finding him in the Temple sitting aside the mix of the teachers and scribes
seemingly they enjoyed setting a scene to elicit facts then unlock the lesson
mostly he listened to them just slightly to the side bar asking few questions
if asked all who heard were astounded at his knowledge in answers for fact
amazed at his exceptional renditions and a curious ability for long past events
due to age he only could rejoinder respectfully if invited by their challenges
all who heard him were astounded by his understanding and answers rendered.

III

Upon their finding him all three engaged in a robust greeting of hugs
there was no recrimination or chastisement or justifiable annoyance
it was a reunion of relief after harboring the parents eternal worst fears
instant reflection between each of faith's strongest familial bonds of union
quite momentary celebration of heartfelt and soul gleaned requisite joinder
assurances secure as radiance of truth known but unspoken with time to go.

Melchior scribe noted abiding sense of calm in words and actions toward each
confidently shown between each and together as one united in familial purpose
though slightly overshadowed by the youth's exercise of unattended independence
his sublimating time as though replicating meditational inspection all self to the good
Son, why have you done this to us;
Your father and I have been looking for you with great anxiety.

Melchior was then told of a less evident yet curiously made remark from the boy
the scribe spy present overheard him say to his parents of their misunderstanding
Why were you looking for me;
Did you not know that I must be in my Father's house,
said with emphasis and intimation it could not be otherwise any contradictory place.

Exiting Temple area in the the middle of both parents he remarked on his absence
his having said did you not know that I would be at my Father's House in a level tone
it was a impromptu response seemingly suggesting no need for incredulous worry
something near-like as in he knew you new and you new he knew without the where
neither spoke in answer as they continued their return through the north facing gate

each now considered what was evident to the boy and later became evident to them
perhaps thinking metaphorically late to the party of seeking truth in God's creations
no pique just celebration calming fears together going forward smiling not looking back
the new man and both his parents were seen as happily comfortable around each other.

IV

Together by three leaving that city of hope to heirs of the Ancient One
a tempest of fears allayed finding him secure in righteous discovery
satisfaction in his dedicated duty attending a most revered obligation
unspoken wonderment at a boy so young so drawn to His house
incidence of pronounced and performed mystery engraved as one.

Once more venturing their difficult life gaining on the caravans place
back to their hearth their friends to each other's comfort and work
previous fears evaporating like a morning dew under a rising sun
having care of their child grown man lost then found virtuous of blame
leaving they anticipated next year's usual ceremonial celebrations
each year a communal feast offering Passover of Jews in Jerusalem
.

Thus the flustering day of the circuitous finding relented
fraternal thoughts moving memories joined eternally
now to families all in future's flowing events
as in meaning by age youth presents
face by grace of unknown wisdom
sure as rule to order all in place
dignity cements grace to face
holy affirmity all in place
the three in finding
Ancient One first
then the boy
for the love
of both
making
three.

Interregnum III

I

In a personal event of subsequence Melchior related on a matter of consequence
he did commune with the Temple collegium while in that Hebraic City of defense,
extemporaneously attending to matters of commerce partial to cost and reward
what's taken and paid for at a variant fair price both low and high for great award.

Malchior sought to learn and better know of him by chief agent scribe evidence
who flowed freely outright about and among chief priests few in need by bribe

we acolytes asked him to relate the evident interplay with those powers that be
quizzical inferences crossed over his aged face some as though stung by bug
relaxing he began to relate all that had transpired as told by attendant scribes.

The great wise man known to kings and courts of the east and west
of the way of Aristocles logic in science of earth, wind, water and fire
speaking of his time at the Temple with words of the known witnesses
in speach he tempered embellishments and as usual spoke calmly.

II

The youth was intently responsive to historic causal events
like seminarians engaged in verbally invigorated meanings
other religious were amazed of his factual knowledge
that of a time or a place of who and what occurred
listening he sought to learn their meanings and feelings.

He cared little for food or flair in discussions quietly debated
others engaged him in what he knew well and quickly related
details of scripture and events in the Book intimately presented
in ways direct and true a marvel to hear no sophistic intent created
no mistake nor truth denied no ornament to romantic place or time.

He expressed himself aided sometimes by furrowed face of curious smiles
with words from the great recorded and piously rewarding Book of Books
all the while by vantage under overhung bisected cypress wood beams
forming a cooler shadowed locus within an outermost Temple side court
not far from the presence of the Ancient One there not seen by mortals
neatly adjacent of theTemple and within the centrality of Scribes and Rabbis
city ultimately encased by an unholy guarded surround gained of pagan power.

Magi's scribe on point quoted him saying I am here to learn of you
to learn of the interpretive ways of scholars or scribes and priests
of historic glories in seeking saving and securing faith and fidelity
wanting to know of the whys and wherefores of pregnant unknowables
expressing vibrant curiosities seemingly beyond his age for understanding
being relaxed he extended kindness and courtesy for the want of knowing
learning by some latent thought in a spell of that his morrowed self sought.

The brilliant late morning sun slowly moved dark lines of shade over all
the boy occasionally to be shadowed under overhanging crossed beams
a carriage of pillar and post nailed with awning tempering yawning heat
doldrums of heavy northern air stifled clear breathing but not clear thought.

He related clear and precise references cited to subject
complexity of discourse did not hinder his want to know
even so his language command was unadorned simplicity
accommodated by some for being a very able biblical student
to others a unsophisticated rustic tolerated as an interesting child
all was a joy in the listening of his words and his ways of confidence.

His attention to detail surprising knowledge seeking truths beyond simplicity
a sense of serenity carried him in complimenting his strength of confidence
noting scribes aids among those gathered would seek to know to believe
he referencing best to believe so that one may know not to suppose
particularly how it was written to the times and ways in The Book.

III

His presentment excluded pacing
mainly sitting or standing aside listening
to intellects to the pious to cynic or skeptic
small groups sitting near on stone stairs or chairs
wooden bench or standing to moving into and out from
none particularly outlandish or commanding in the group
all seeking insights to exact some little known fact or folly
to anoint themselves calling forth some union in Biblical history
of grand glorious schemes and monumental failures agonizes replete
always the hope and the miraculous possibilities to the fantastic in the promise
memories and meaning ere long lost in past repairs here regained and made anew.

When asked he spoke each word with conformity maintaining values of The Book
many admitted of the boy's knowing words of ways by fact equitably judged fair
of his questions or offered answers from his mouth all came with humiliity's care.

During his presence discourse rendered lively spontaneity
usual rivalries dissipated like hot afternoons cloud curlicues
excited by a uniquely gifted fire with vigor infuseing each subject
igniting interests inflamed by not complimenting pride seeking truth
meanings were voided of jealoulsies's scowles hiding in hateful smiles.

He was most interested in the how and why of the way they thought
discourse of participants was variously serious to humorous all adept
engaging each other drawing upon events of The Book to what it 'ment
some seemed to enjoy having the boy extemporaneously marshal facts
understanding events and details often to their most elevated accuracies.

When coaxed his calm renditions bemused and delighted those in seminar
a rustic with unadorned command of historical compositions unexaggerated
while Scribes and Rabbis cobbled together meanings for that revealed truth
their guides for civilizing Judaic consequences by Torah and all of The Book
as how the chance to make good or ill imprinted all consent that seeks belief.

The boy listened intently to all the stories and measured inferences embedded
that the Ancient One's love of them is sealed by covenants reigning supreme
this too it's grand intensity and complexity of laws and statutes and customs
they seek the road of some salvation in act and thought and their singular faith.

Melchior's subsidized scribe recounted how the boy's parents eventually found him
in the finding they did not marvel at his independence of mind or his failure to inform

neither commended his unforeseen absence nor gruffly affirm their warranted worry
there was no accusatory exchange or admonitions or reprimands issued between them.

No one had notice of his calling or knew of his attraction to the core of its God center
the scribe noted him say he became engrossed in the expressions and depths of faith
was enjoined by the meditative excitement and interaction between masters students
enthralled by their needs to hold dear their well studied singularly revered Ancient One.

I

They left the Temple area to regain joinder with their caravan now third day out
last words heard between the boy and Mary and Joseph were odd by degree
assurance by him saying did you not know I would be at my Father's house
evoking no vocal reproach rather a seemingly worried acknowledgement
together the three turned a close corner disappearing from loyal scribe's view
making again it's foundational truth of this city of hope being the waking dream
a City of Hope charged on a wish and a favor both containing substance in faith.

II

Melchior now coursing his near final stretch
reconciling there was soon death to fetch
then a sign at wedding events in Cana
it began prophecies now rendering
enforcing its truth wins in the end
learning by reports transcribed
at times Melchiour's eyes
of resolute expression
to final acceptance.

The Wedding

1

His cherished father Joseph succumbed to a not uncommon work related death in place
then falling from a 2nd story cedar beam and found lying on his back near a resting dove
laying on a soft mound of sandy garden fill made lighter by the face of calm expression
clear eyes in the eternal gaze directed upward toward the sunlight of the world above
countenance of his weathered face that of the gentle and righteous man that he was
it was reported that he was seen grasping hands against his heart expressing pain
he would be sorely missed by his many friends who worked years alongside him.
a disaster by combinations of wet beams and his sudden bent over chest pains
leaving late from the second story of a wooden cross beamed Esdraela building
by that employer he was a well respected and experienced carpenter of service
news came hard on that small family at a dangerous time in a commonplace

First the congregate sadness then interment according to Judiac protocol
always its suddenness harboring the grief of the loss of physical presence
recall of intimate exchanges and concerns of all this and more before that fall
through it all one could sense calm resolve strengthened by constance of faith.

II

Consequent of Gaspar's and Balthassar's scribes are letters and dispatches
Melchior keen to emphasize that he be rightly informed of any weighty event
seventeen years informations within satchels relating to him were all tranquil
the sudden loss of Joseph reckoned that which would become extraordinary

In the time before this event there were no reports of outstanding exceptionalism
indeed the intervening years were those of sporadic constance of commonality
at best any reports however maintained became fewer and farther between
other than a respectful pious nondiscript average and hard working family
besides the family's well reputed reputation and of their helping others
nothing to evidence any sight of Jesus being other than a good man
a loving and loyal relations demonstrated toward family and friends
now wearing grief strengthened resolve to maintain Mary's safety.

Past private mourning both Jesus and Mother attended a wedding at Cana
a ceremony especial for Joseph's brother's niece being youthful and bright
an event which would evidence an extrasensory transformative manifestation
something of a beginning quietly executed at a mother's request then to ignite
it was his mother's first social outing from the security of their quiet home area
together to a familial celebration of joyful union months after Joseph's demise.

I

Now something of significance at a wedding feast in the celebratory Tabernacle tent
all reports prior showed Jesus being uniquely commendable in words and actions
to date a decent honest helpful man of no bad habit or self-centered permissiveness
no predict of royal presentations though an exceptionally honest and faithful friend
an unpretentious man of reserved confidence in manner of speech or temperament.

II

Then there came to be the report of wedding events in the Galilean village of Cana
first hand reports by a scribe's meeting with an attending friend of a cousin's sister
a woman of trusted probity who recently aided Mary thru immediate home needs
all that day assisting family catering aids hastening food and drinks to the guests
she could directly relate that which occurred concerning the events at the cisterns.

In whispering glances all enjoyed their celebration of fidelity's marriage place
some number of festive guests moved by the rules of Abraham's joyful music
the swirls and twirls by sounds of fipple flute, drums, lutes and lyre for dances
communally danced once with his mother near others holding virtue's carriage
he spoke in rustic ease with guests including several of his attending friends
words of him becoming a teacher gathering mixed acolytus of different trends.

Catered by the guests a few dressed in handmade finery showing some lace
well prepared fish or lamb for a solid choice of food in proportional amounts
breads massaged into basic shapes well browned some of colored trace
vegetables and fruits in bowls and baskets guarded from animals jump.

Olive oil was plentiful and liberally used on flesh cooked or skin colored
beans, dates, nuts readily available not so for delicacies of oyster and caviar
there were congratulatory tips of wine and innocently toasted boasts lightly boiled
sooner than expected there developed concerns regarding the wine bought from afar.

Most unmindful to cater and the later gatherings of wedding guests
became obvious to the wine servers and was unknown to the groom
cisterns holding the serving wine near drained by empty cups on desks
food and festive activities and dry heat conspired in the wines total doom.

Informed the groom hurried to the empty jars fearful of confirming the worst
once known his mood turned to worry exasperation and to his own faults
the bride arrived joining her husband lamenting of the party loss so serious
a bad omen reared its ugly possibility of presence ending in water and salts

III

Then it happened that which was invisible suddenly became visible
what was contained wondrously became the substance of something new

the few nearby who heard and witnessed what was impossible were indivisible
a superlative new unheard of or ever witnessed manipulation of natural substances
it was an event of unnatural transmutation causing a recalibration of changing elements.

Quietly conversing nearby were several local attendants and Mary's city friend
heeding concerns all clearly heard his mother say to him they have no wine
instantly he knew what she wanted him to do without her finishing any request
demurring by oddly saying his hour has not yet come as though he were elsewhere.

So then it happened after she telling the servers to do whatever he tells you
thinking of course the servers would be told to go out and locate more wine
expecting by some infringement he told the servers to top up jars of water
that accomplished he instructed them to dip serving jars into that same water
without notice otherwise he told them to serve what they thought was water
jars and jugs are not colored to reflect wines and water simply reflects darkly
astonishment jumped when finally served it was revealed as the best of wines.

When the headwaiter tasted the water that had become the best of wine
excited in relief he whispered to the groom for him to proudly announce
boasting of its quality without knowing from where to came or how
the telling by the groom received numerous accolades readily accepted
he presumably in jest having saved the best of wine until the last of festivities
ignorant of its true source and skeptically dismissing any mysterious attribution
except for servers Jesus' entourage and a mother's requested gift from her son.

IV

When Melchiour received report of what happened he was every bit excited
before the servers returned, Jesus, his mother and his invited group had gone
to the scribe spy this event without stir was portent of greater changes to come
on notice to Balthazar and Gaspar as Melchior described impossible being possible
Melchior then tasked me to Jerusalem to learn more of this preternatural transformation.

Melchior then began to take a closer look informed by past theology and sciences
recalling the abstractions of Diogenes Laertius' philosophy of atoms becoming all
again the unknowable Ancient One engineering entanglements of smallest particles
what of all matter forever in flux makes this man some conjured gift of the Ancient One
later evidence convinced him without doubt of Jesus being that called prophetic new king.

I

As Melchiors esteemed acolyte I was tasked to seek out Jesus
this new king's revealed teaching now made certain in Judea
too soon great where terrible actions and events unfolded
I report things and thoughts with truth closely held
I now have hope nor want it otherwise inside
in him, through him, with him hope resides

for you and me to never set it aside
grant my scribe spy's are yours
to seek that obvious in faith
with suffering to become
a true love of Jesus
the new king
for ages
to be.

(Acolyte's Choice)

Thirty some years past near last Caesar Augustus' reign
I traveled to many lands as royal counsel to tasks yet realized
seeking truths or divining for answers of unimaginable strain
historic military strategies to fundamental science conceptualized.

to leave quiescent gardens seeking to unravel the unknown
to not be set aside in a royal tower and a world cloistered
to test self serving needs and not cause love to flee unborn
to seek what becomes The Way of a new born king not foisted
to know a light so lovingly bright it repels immortal darkness away.

II

Melchior now tasked me, Tangentio, to learn more of this Jesus
a pilgrimage for prophetic truths in understanding a beginning
to learn of living in a promised new age of a promised new being
testing logic and reason's mistresses not as a policeman of faith.

Bent by age he lamented ever to meet as sure a king such as this
true fulfillment of prophecy, exactly, confidently, magnificently bold
understanding faithfully now making unassured all relying on gold
prescribing aid for a new king of lowly birth perhaps of ignominious end
a much sought after figuration carrying time by its prophesy never to unfold.

Once saying it is fact he traveled to centers of learning and palaces of wonder
allied to various religions divining powers for ill to evil or good to benevolent
rulers mercurial and unstable commanding by force, fear, division and confusion
others more beneficent ruling by equitable considerations and measures in laws
some unbalanced and heavenly dependent on never enough and the almighty sword
Melchior's key was to gain knowledge in the doing and don'ts of science and philosophy
to gain and maintain the need and values of the knowing all to aid of the lingering unknown
to fight the good fight without the intrusion of shame or false challenge toward a fool's power.

My status as a scribe required hard travel in simple clothing with value hidden
tasked to report back any events of him evidencing any actions of royal prophecy
ever protected and aided by a healthy network of mentor's friends and paid agents
no longer an acolyte rather a non-descriptive scribe seeking information from teachers.

I

I, Tangentio, would now write of the greatest happenings that would ever be told
those chapters written to my mentor of events beyond any ever known
to ignite a fire of hope so bright as may invigorate all upon this earth

one who would expose the magnificence of the Ancient One
to show this world it's only road to eternal salvation
to reimagine creation as it once had been
giving truth to faith in what is possible
showing The Way open to all
that and more of fact
casting darkness
farther away
by the light
Almighty
so near
now.

- Adhaesio Tangentio -
(The Way)

Printed in the United States
by Baker & Taylor Publisher Services